Ages 5–8

50 SPELLING ACTIVITIES

FOR ANY SPELLING PROGRAMME

Letter Patterns, Spelling, Word Building, Games, Sound Patterns, Rhyme, Word Sorts, Magazine Search

Published by Prim-Ed Publishing

www.prim-ed.com

Foreword

50 Spelling Activities contains a variety of fun activities which can be used with any spelling list or programme.

The activities are designed to provide opportunities for children to practise their spelling words and use a variety of strategies to develop understanding and recall. The majority of the activities can be completed within twenty minutes, making them ideal for the Group and Independent Work element of the Literacy Hour. Activities can be photocopied onto coloured or plain card and laminated for protection. As each activity can be used with any spelling list, children can, to some extent, choose the activities they wish to use, to help develop both their learning of conventional spelling and their independence.

50 Spelling Activities also contains:

- Spelling Activity Checklist to record activities undertaken by individual children;
- Have-A-Go Spelling Sheet to encourage children to attempt to spell unfamiliar words; and
- Curriculum Links to illustrate how the activities fit into the English National Curriculum.

Also in this series: **50 Spelling Activities** (Middle/Upper) Ages 7 – 12

Contents

Curriculum Links		ii
Spelling Activity Checklist		iii
Have-a-Go sheet		iv
Activity 1	Which Word?	1
Activity 2	Word Strips	2
Activity 3	Jigsaw Words	3
Activity 4	Spiral Words	4
Activity 5	Word Sorts	5
Activity 6	Wiggly Worm	6
Activity 7	New Words	7
Activity 8	Word Wheel	8
Activity 9	Fill the Gaps	
Activity 10	Look, Say, Cover, Write, Check	9
Activity 11	Patterns	
Activity 12	Word Building—1	10
Activity 13	Word Building—2	
Activity 14	Spelling Fold-a-book	11
Activity 15	Word Ladder	12
Activity 16	Secret Code	
Activity 17	Write, Write, Write!	13
Activity 18	Antonyms and Synonyms	14
Activity 19	Word Guess	
Activity 20	Alphabet Search	15
Activity 21	Tricky Word Sort	16
Activity 22	Small Words in Big Words	
Activity 23	Read and Draw	17
Activity 24	Word Hunt	
Activity 25	Word Worm	18
Activity 26	Boggle Words	
Activity 27	Word Hospital	19
Activity 28	Word Search	
Activity 29	Leap Frog	20
Activity 30	Magazine Hunt	21
Activity 31	Word Grid	22
Activity 32	Rhyming Words	23
Activity 33	Word Detective!	
Activity 34	Decorated Words	24
Activity 35	Naughts and Crosses	
Activity 36	Tricky Words	25
Activity 37	Computer Game Spelling	
Activity 38	Make Your Own Bookmark	26
Activity 39	Funny Phrases	
Activity 40	Join the Letters	27
Activity 41	Spelling Sums	28
Activity 42	Jumbled Words	
Activity 43	Dominoes	29
Activity 44	Spelling Questions	30
Activity 45	Blast Off!	
Activity 46	Partner Testing	31
Activity 47	Wordo!	
Activity 48	Hello Hippo!	32
Activity 49	Fish	33
Activity 50	Snail Concentration	34

Curriculum Links

50 Spelling Activities provides a wide range of fun activities, giving children opportunities to practise their spelling words whilst encouraging the development of strategies crucial to the learning of conventional spelling. The activities in *50 Spelling Activities* will encourage pupils to demonstrate the following Writing Programme of Study objectives of the English National Curriculum.

Book	Year Group	Subject	Curriculum Strand	Content Objectives	
Lower	KS1	English	En3 Writing	4.	Spelling
					Pupils should be taught:
					Spelling Strategies
				4b	use their knowledge of sound-symbol relationships and phonological patterns
				4c	recognise and use simple spelling patterns
				4d	write common letter strings
				4e	spell common words
				4f	spell words with common prefixes and inflectional endings
					Checking Spelling
				4h	use their knowledge of word families and other words
Middle/ Upper	KS2	English	En3 Writing	4.	Spelling
					Pupils should be taught:
					Spelling Strategies
				4a	to sound out phonemes
				4b	to analyse words into syllables and other known words
				4c	to apply knowledge of spelling conventions
				4d	to use knowledge of common letter strings, visual patterns and analogies
				4f	to revise and build upon their knowledge of words and spelling patterns
					Morphology
				4g	the meaning, use and spelling of common prefixes and suffixes
				4h	the spelling of words with inflectional endings
				4i	the relevance of word families, roots and origins of words
				4j	the use of appropriate terminology, including vowel, consonant, homophone and syllable

Spelling Activity Checklist

Name _____

Activity	Completed			Comment
1				
2				
3				
4				
5				
6				
7				
8				
9				
10				
11				
12				
13				
14				
15				
16				
17				
18				
19				
20				
21				
22				
23				
24				
25				

Activity	Completed			Comment
26				
27				
28				
29				
30				
31				
32				
33				
34				
35				
36				
37				
38				
39				
40				
41				
42				
43				
44				
45				
46				
47				
48				
49				
50				

Having trouble spelling a word?
Have-a-Go

- [ ] Sound it out.
- [ ] Write it down.
- [ ] Look at the word you are trying to write.
- [ ] Does it look right?
- [ ] Try again—and maybe again.
- [ ] Check with your teacher.

The best way for me to remember how to spell a word is to …

_____

Remember: Sound it out and have at least three attempts at spelling an unknown word.

Having trouble spelling a word?
Have-a-Go

- [ ] Sound it out.
- [ ] Write it down.
- [ ] Look at the word you are trying to write.
- [ ] Does it look right?
- [ ] Try again—and maybe again.
- [ ] Check with your teacher.

The best way for me to remember how to spell a word is to …

_____

Remember: Sound it out and have at least three attempts at spelling an unknown word.

Activity 1   **Which Word?**

🐾 Find a partner with the same spelling words.
🐾 Choose a word from your list.
🐾 Start by telling your partner the first letter of your word.
🐾 How many clues before your partner guesses your word?

Activity 2

Word Strips

Example

og | l | d | f | j | h

Note to teachers:
- Write a word family ending on the short strips and initial letters on the long strips before photocopying and laminating.
- Cut along the dotted lines.
- Slide letter strips through the slits to make words.

Prim-Ed Publishing ~ www.prim-ed.com

Activity 3

Jigsaw Words

- Choose a spelling word.
- Write the beginning of the word on one jigsaw piece.
- Write the end of the word on the other.
- Do the same for seven others.
- Cut them out, mix them up, and try to join them together.

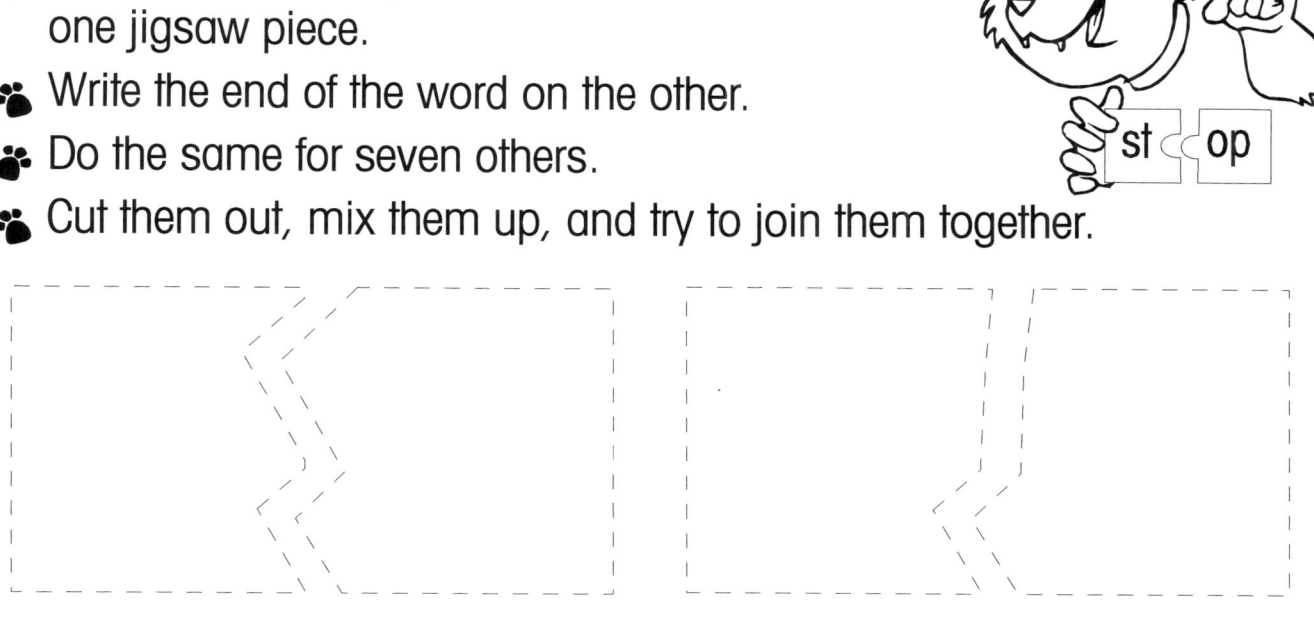
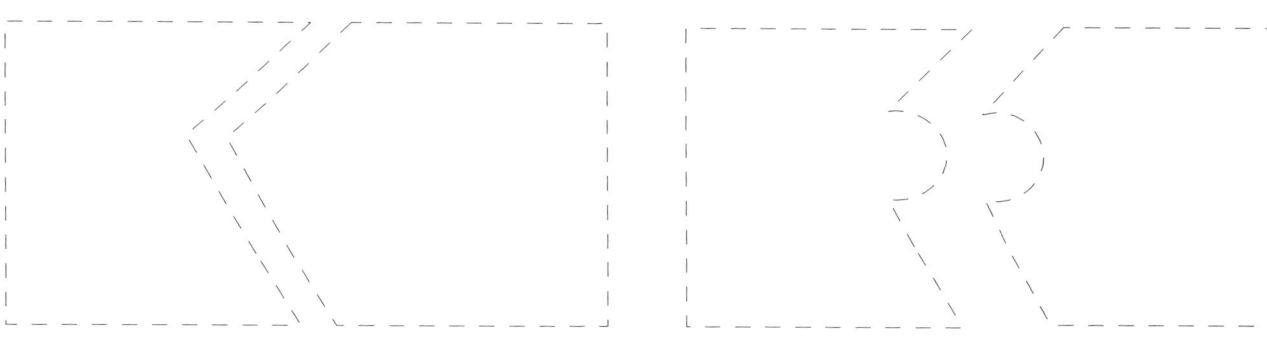
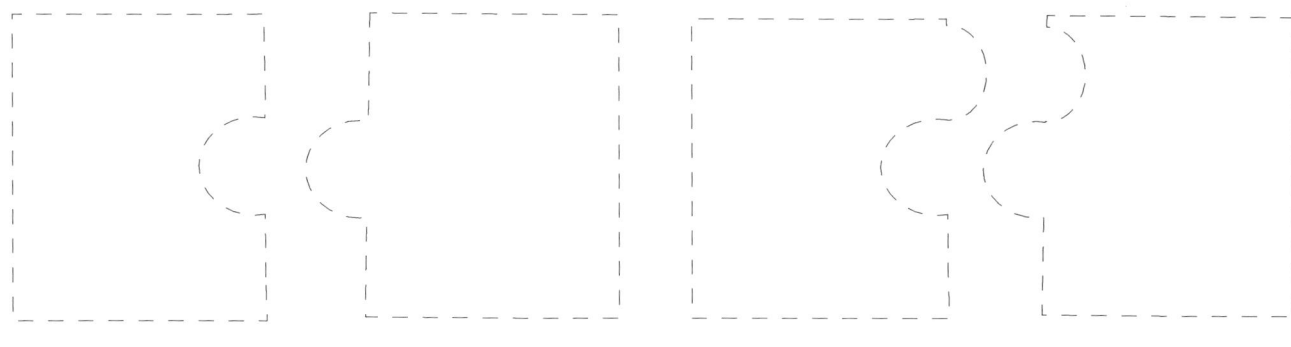
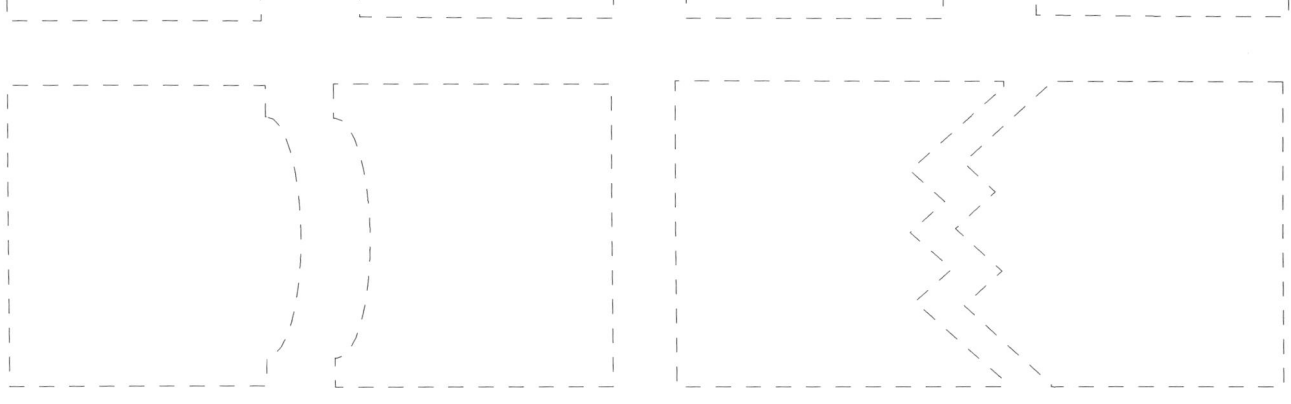

Activity 4

Spiral Words

- Write your spelling words in bright colours along the spiral.
- Cut along the dotted lines to make a curly paper spiral.
- Hang the spiral in your classroom!

Activity 5

Word Sorts

Sort your spelling words and write them in the correct box.
Words may be written more than once.

Words with two letters

Words you can draw a picture for

Words with three or more letters

Words that rhyme

Activity 6

Wiggly Worm

- Write some of your spelling words in the boxes.
- Cut them out and glue them onto the page to make a word worm.
- Pass your word worm to a friend.
  Can he or she read all of the words in your worm?

Prim-Ed Publishing ~ www.prim-ed.com

Activity 7

New Words

Name ☐

My new word is
☐

My word written

looks like
☐

- My word begins with the letter(s) ☐
- My word ends with the letter(s) ☐
- The middle letter is ☐

- My word written small looks like
☐
- My word written in colour looks like
☐

- Cover your word.
- Colour a balloon every time you write your new word correctly.

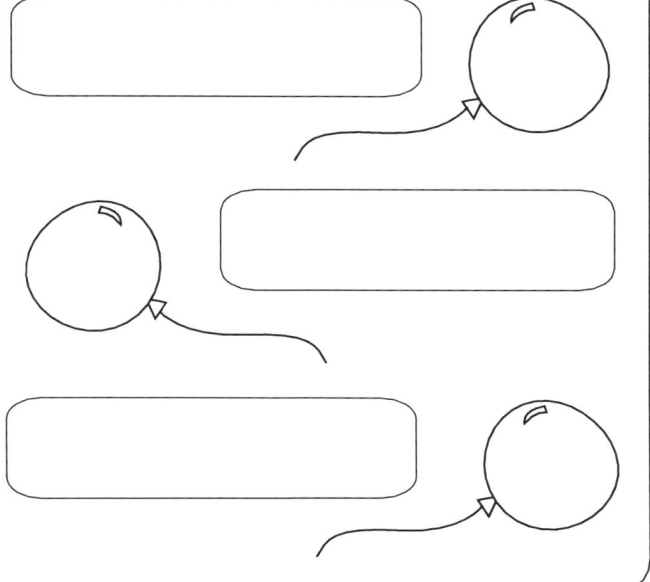

- Can you draw your word or somebody doing your word?
☐

Prim-Ed Publishing ~ www.prim-ed.com   50 Spelling Activities   7

Activity 8 **Word Wheel**

🐾 Write one of the following sets of letters into the parts of the wheel.

r	b	d	s
t	f	p	w

th	wh	br	sh
dr	st	ch	tr

🐾 On a separate piece of paper, write a word that begins with each of the letters on the wheel.

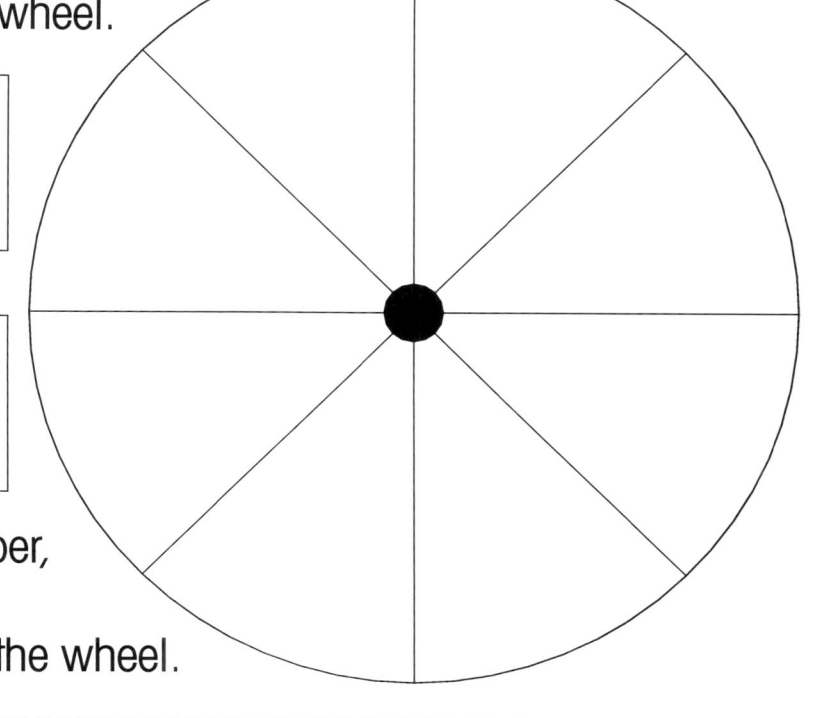

Activity 9 **Fill the Gaps**

🐾 Find a partner with the same spelling words.

🐾 Choose a word from the list.

🐾 Start by giving your partner the first letter of one of the words.

🐾 How many clues before your partner guesses the word?

Prim-Ed Publishing ~ www.prim-ed.com

Activity 10 — **Look, Say, Cover, Write, Check**

- Write five spelling words in the first column of boxes and follow the directions in the pictures for each word.

Look

Say

Cover

Write

Check

Activity 11 — **Patterns**

- Choose six spelling words that look and sound different.
- Write at least four more words with the same letter pattern.
- For example, shop: shut, shed, shoe.

Word	Words with the same letter pattern

Activity 12 — **Word Building—1**

🐾 Choose five spelling words.
🐾 Make new words by adding an ending.

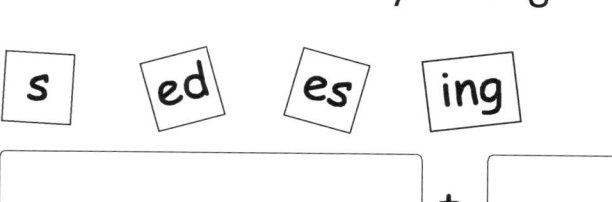

s   ed   es   ing

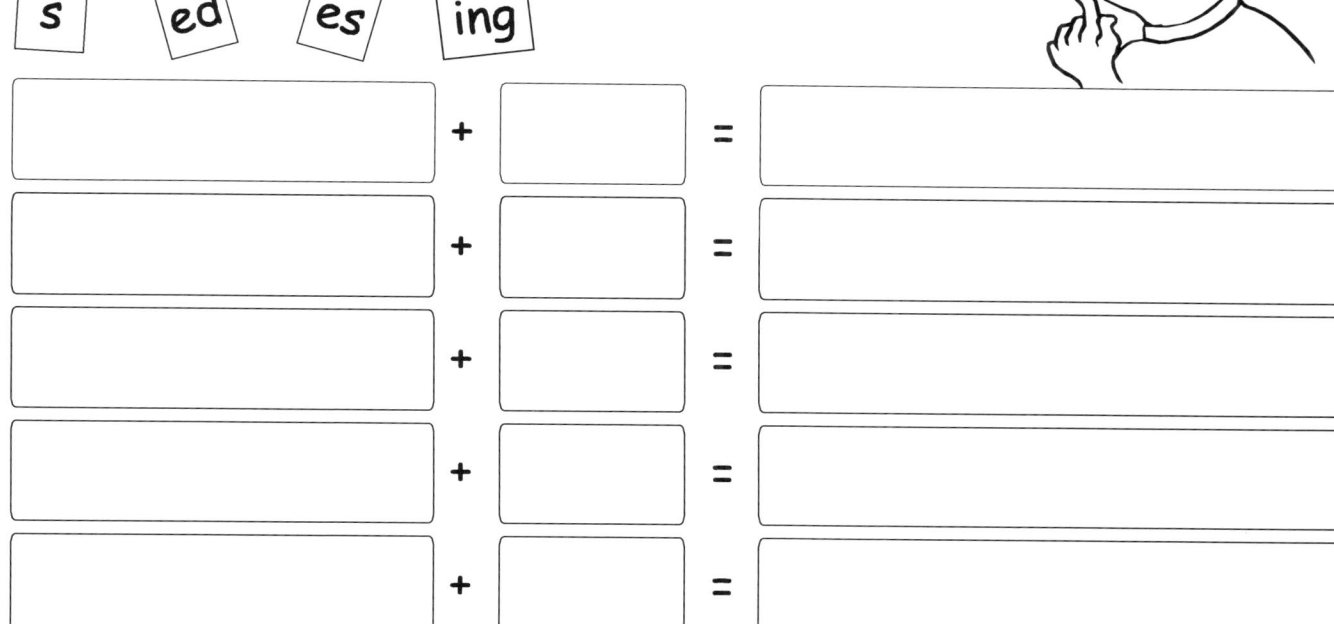

☐ + ☐ = ☐
☐ + ☐ = ☐
☐ + ☐ = ☐
☐ + ☐ = ☐
☐ + ☐ = ☐

Activity 13 — **Word Building—2**

🐾 Choose five spelling words.
🐾 Make new words by adding an ending.

y   er   ly   less   ful

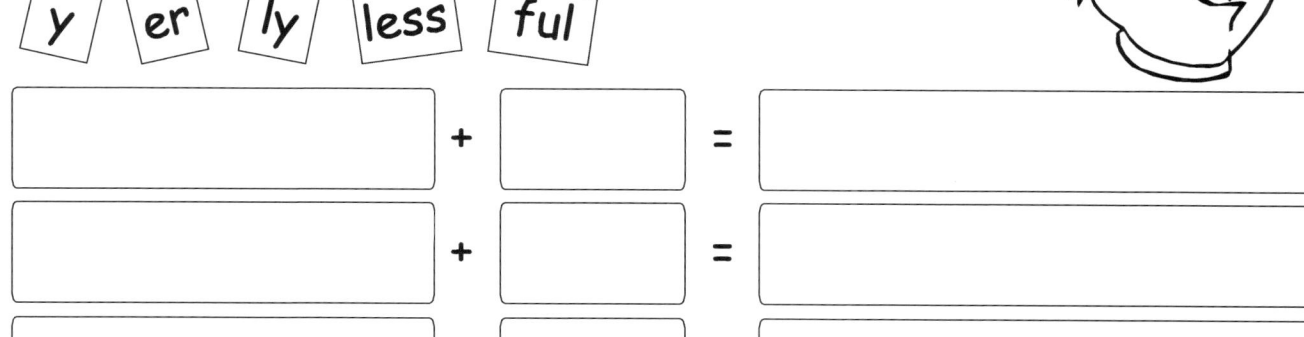
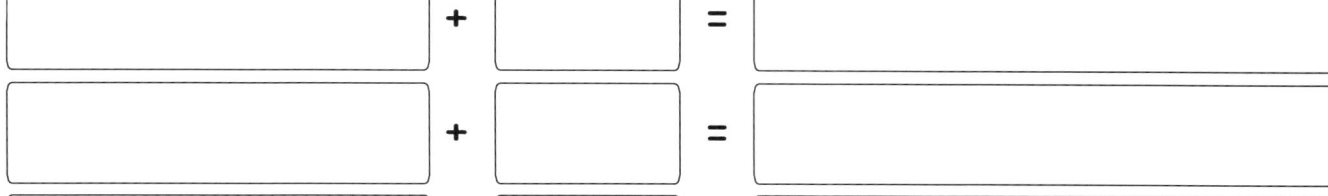

☐ + ☐ = ☐
☐ + ☐ = ☐
☐ + ☐ = ☐
☐ + ☐ = ☐
☐ + ☐ = ☐

Prim-Ed Publishing ~ www.prim-ed.com

Activity 14 — Spelling Fold-a-book

Write five spelling words. Draw a picture for each.

Choose your two favourite colours. Write each word in one colour. Trace over each word with the other.

Write your words from the easiest to spell to the hardest to spell.

_____'s

Little

Book of Spelling Words

Activity 15 — Word Ladder

🐾 Write your words to make a ladder.

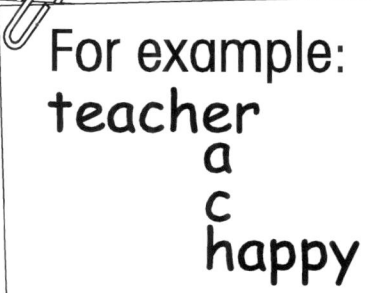

For example:
teacher
    a
    c
happy

✏ You may use extra words but check carefully that they are spelt correctly.

Activity 16 — Secret Code

🐾 Choose three spelling words. Write the letters found in each word underneath a picture. (Not in order!)

🐾 Use the pictures to write the words in your new secret code.

🐾 Give your code to a friend. Can he or she solve it?

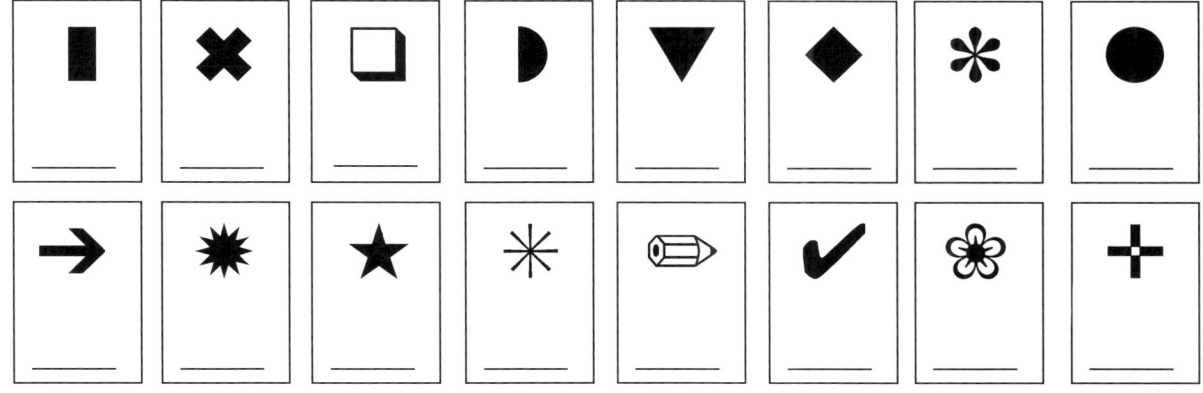

Your code: _____

Solution: _____

Activity 17 — Write, Write, Write!

- How many times can you write your spelling words in these shapes?
- Choose a different word for each shape.

Activity 18 — Antonyms and Synonyms

- Antonyms are words with the opposite meaning.
- Synonyms are words with the same meaning.
- Write five list words and find an antonym and a synonym for each.

Spelling Words	Antonyms	Synonyms

Activity 19 — Word Guess!

- Choose one of your partner's spelling words. Write a dash for each letter. Your partner must now guess the first letter. If his or her guess is correct, write that letter on the line. If his or her guess is incorrect, colour one of the boxes in the grid. Your partner must guess the word before the grid is coloured!

Game 1

Game 2

Game 3

Game 4

Activity 20 — Alphabet Search

🐾 **Write words that begin with each letter of the alphabet.**
(For an extra challenge, try to find words which are all about one topic; for example, space, summer, animals or food.)

a	n
b	o
c	p
d	q
e	r
f	s
g	t
h	u
i	v
j	w
k	x
l	y
m	z

Activity 21 — Tricky Word Sort

- Sort your spelling words and write them in the correct box.
- Words may be written more than once.

Words with two syllables

Words that are a noun (name of person, place or thing)

Words that end in a vowel

Words that begin with two consonants like 'sh', 'tr' or 'ch'

Activity 22 — Small Words in Big Words

- Write five spelling words.
  (OR ask your teacher to write five tricky words.)
- How many small words can you find?

Word	Small Words

Activity 23 — **Read and Draw**

- Select five list words and draw a picture for each in the boxes.
- See if a friend can guess and spell each word.

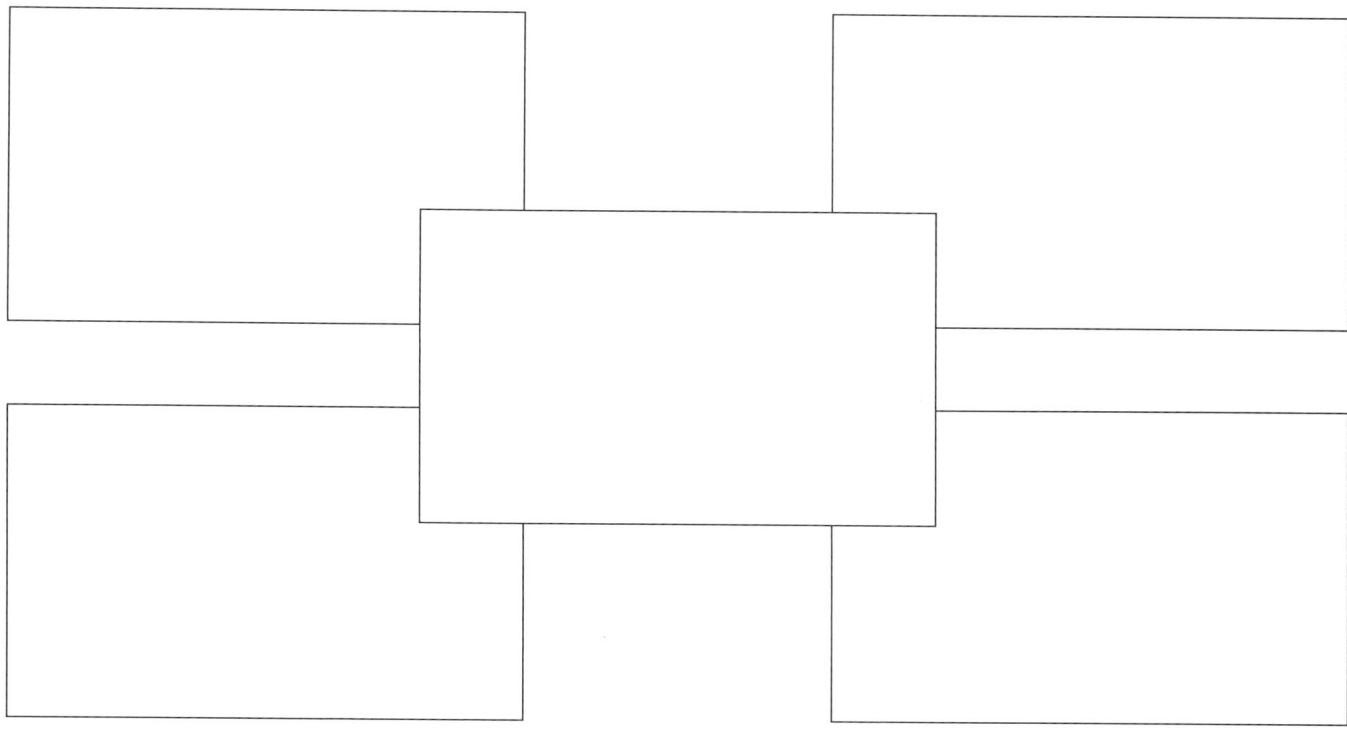

Activity 24 — **Word Hunt**

- Choose five spelling words.
- Using a book you have been reading in class, see if any of your words have been used. If so, how many times? Keep a tally!

Word	Tally	Total

Activity 25 — Word Worm

- Write your spelling words as a word worm.
- Pass your word worm to a friend.
- Can they find all of your words?

Activity 26 — Boggle Words

- Circle 16 letters in the sound list. Write each of the circled letters into a box in the grid.
- On a separate piece of paper, write as many words as you can using the letters in the grid. You can only write words with letters that can be joined up, down or diagonally.

a	c	d	r
i	f	o	x
y	l	p	e
r	s	a	t

Example: drop

Sound list

a	a	e	e	i	i	o
o	u	u	t	r	s	n
m	p	f	l	b	c	d
g	j	h	q	z	k	v
w	x	y	l	t	s	r

Activity 27 — Word Hospital

🐾 Use the word hospital to 'fix up' spelling words you often misspell! Draw an x-ray of your word.

Is this how the word should look?

🐾 Write the word as many times as you can in its hospital bed.

🐾 How will you remember to spell the word?

Activity 28 — Word Search

🐾 Make your own word search using eight spelling words.

🐾 Pass your word search to a friend to do. Can he or she find all of your words?

_____   _____

_____   _____

_____   _____

_____   _____

🐾 Use these letters to fill in the leftover squares.

b c d f g h j k m n
p q r s t v w x y z

Activity 29

Leap Frog

- Write a spelling word in the first lily pad.
- In the next lily pad, write a word which begins with the final letter of the word in lily pad 1.
- Repeat until you reach the end. Don't fall in!

START

FINISH

Prim-Ed Publishing ~ www.prim-ed.com   *50 Spelling Activities*   20

Activity 30 — **Magazine Hunt**

- Search through magazines to find your spelling words.
- Cut out the words you find and glue them below.
- How many spelling words did you find?

I found ☐ spelling words!

Activity 31

Word Grid

- Make a word using two of the sounds below.
- Write the word onto the grid and tick the sounds you used.
- Make as many words as you can without using the same sounds twice.

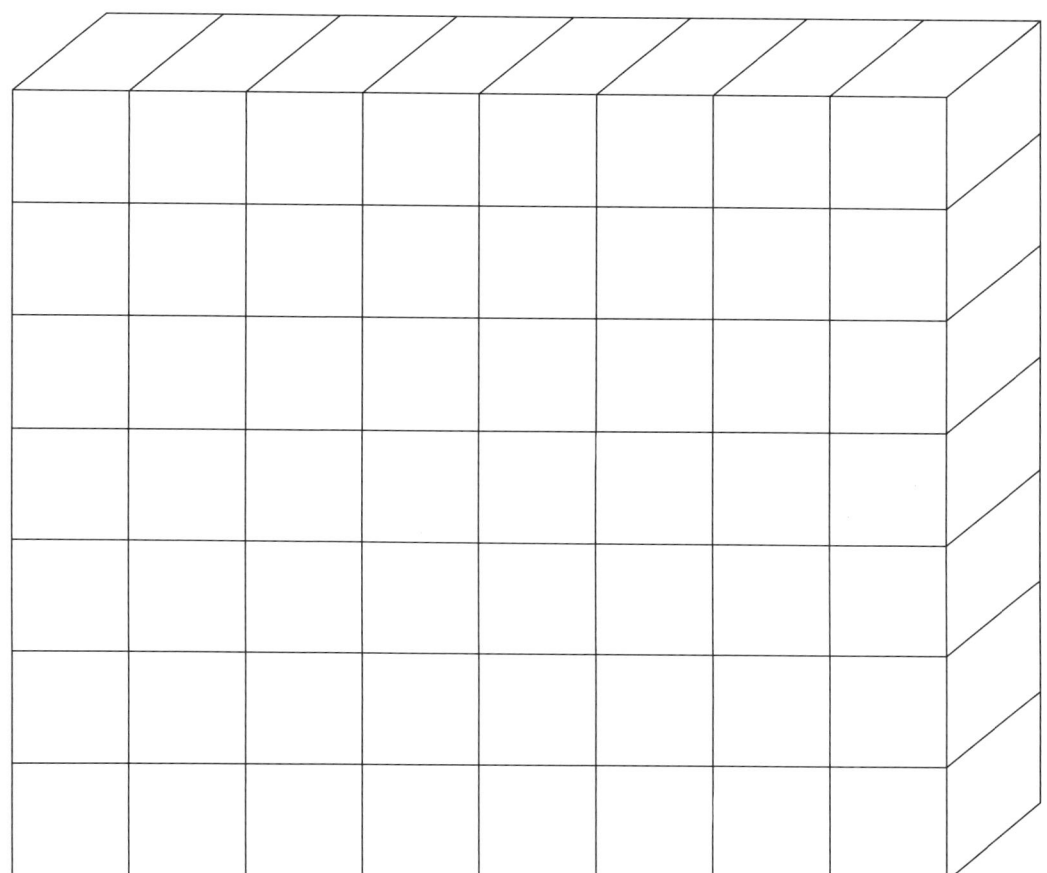

Beginnings
- y
- m
- b
- t
- h
- c
- p
- sh
- ch
- st
- cr
- pl
- cl
- tr

Endings
- et
- op
- ow
- ip
- ap
- ow
- ew
- ig
- al
- ay
- an
- ug
- ut
- ed

Activity 32 — **Rhyming Words**

- Write five spelling words.
- Write as many rhyming words as you can.

Activity 33 — **Word Detective!**

- Write six spelling words on the lines below.
- Circle the vowels in red.
- Circle the consonants in blue.
- Cross out the silent letters.

Write a sentence using as many words from the list as you can.

Activity 34

Decorated Words

- Write five spelling words in pencil in each box.
- Draw around each letter.
- Rub out the pencil words you started with.
- Decorate the remaining shape.

Activity 35

Noughts and Crosses

- Choose five spelling words with a common sound.
- Ask a partner to do the same for a different sound.

In this example, one player used 'sh-' words, and the other '-all' words. The first person to get three words in a row wins!

call	wall	~~ship~~
ball	~~she~~	
~~shock~~		

Activity 36 — **Tricky Words**

🐾 Can you spell two words that fit each pattern?

b__ __ __	__e__	__ __ __t	a__

🐾 Now make up your own tricky pattern and give to a friend.

Activity 37 — **Computer Game Spelling**

🐾 How many words can you make using a letter from each panel in the computer game?

Panel 1: f, b, s, w, c, p, l, d, r
Panel 2: a, e, i, o, u
Panel 3: p, m, n, t, g, d

Activity 38 — # Make Your Own Bookmark

- Use coloured pencils to write five spelling words on this bookmark. Be as creative as you can!
- Colour the border and cut along the dotted lines to finish your bookmark.

Activity 39 — # Funny Phrases

- Write funny phrases using the letters of your spelling words.
  For example, pig – pigs in goo.

Activity 40   **Join the Letters**

🐾 Write your spelling words in the space shuttle.
🐾 Join the letters in the stars to make each word.
   (Hint: You can use the letters more than once.)

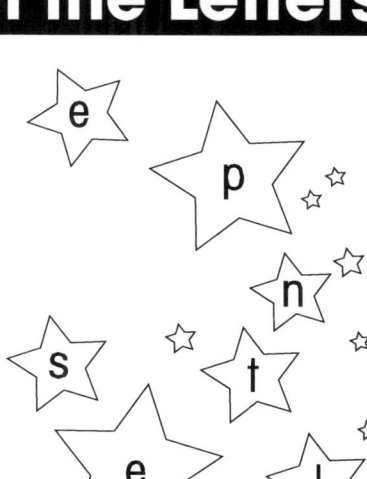

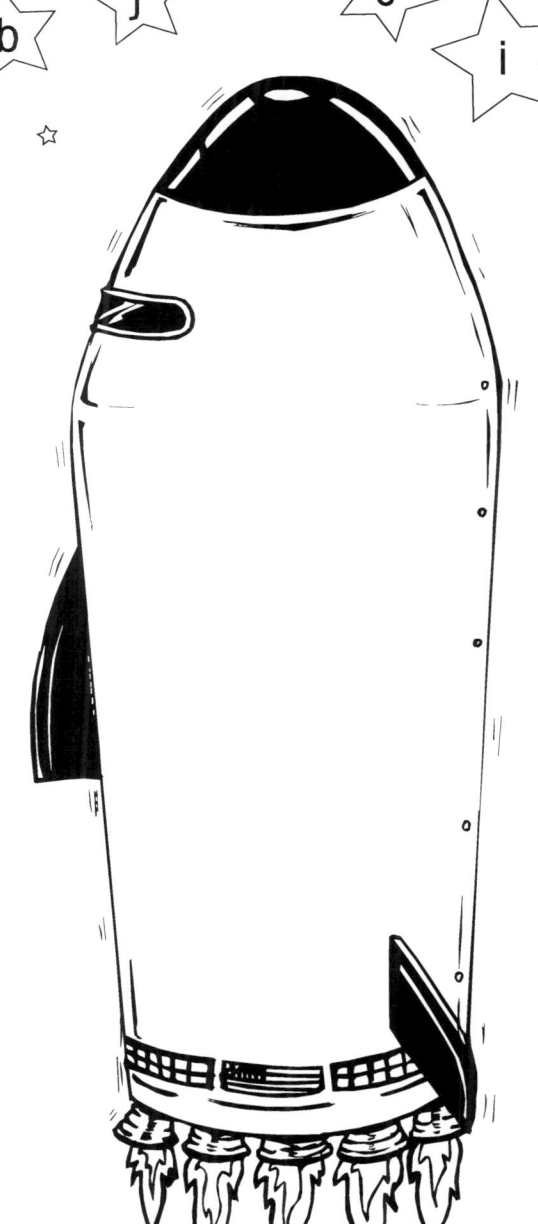

Prim-Ed Publishing ~ www.prim-ed.com   *50 Spelling Activities*   27

Activity 41

Spelling Sums

- Choose five spelling words.
- Write them in the long boxes.
- Make them into spelling sums.

  For example, [b] + [end] = [bend]

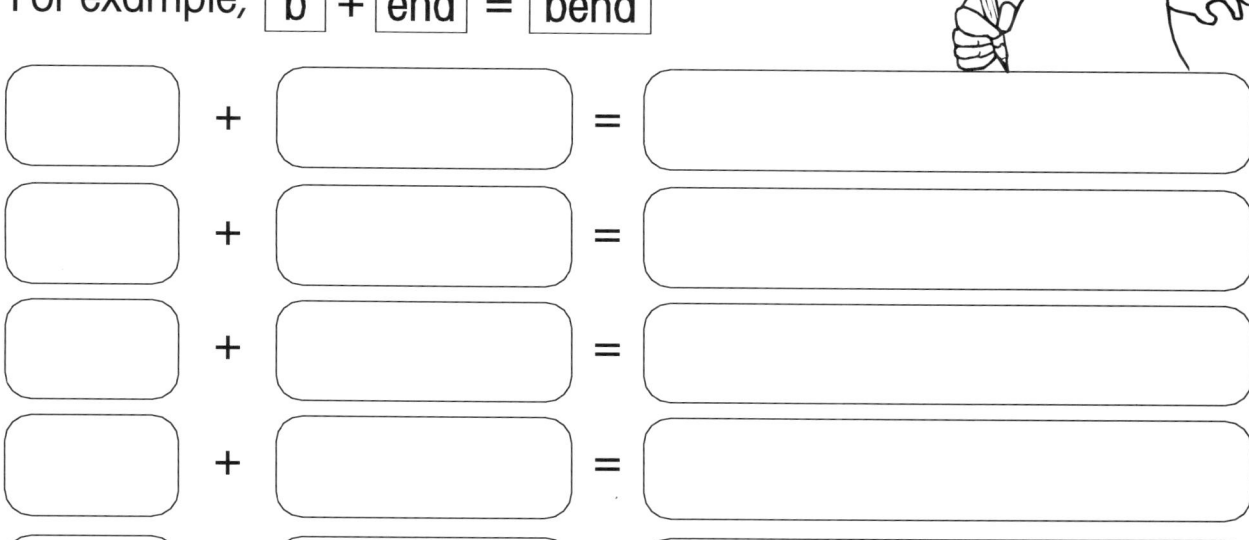

[ ] + [ ] = [ ]

[ ] + [ ] = [ ]

[ ] + [ ] = [ ]

[ ] + [ ] = [ ]

[ ] + [ ] = [ ]

Activity 42

Jumbled Words

- Choose five spelling words.
- Give them to a friend to solve.
- Jumble each word and write it below.
- What was his or her score?  / 5

Jumbled	Unjumbled

Activity 43

Dominoes

- Play dominoes by matching a word beginning on one domino with a word ending on another.

ock	sh		in	tr		et	fl		am	wh
it	pl		ant	br		on	th		ing	st
at	fr		om	dr		an	gl		og	gr
ot	pr		ad	qu		ig	str		ip	wr
up	p		ag	s		op	t		ap	w
ix	z		ut	b		ox	f		ed	d
ee	c		eg	h		ook	l		ome	m
ish	j		y	gn		eed	n		ick	r
ent	v		im	w		elf	bl		ow	shr
ell	spr		ill	spl		oo	thr		ew	ch

Activity 44

Spelling Questions

🐾 Write five spelling words below.

Spelling Word	How many letters does it have?	Can you think of a rhyming word?	Clap the syllables. How many?	Can you draw a picture of the word?

Activity 45

Blast Off!

🐾 Choose a spelling word for a friend to guess.

🐾 Draw a dash for each letter in the word in the rocket.

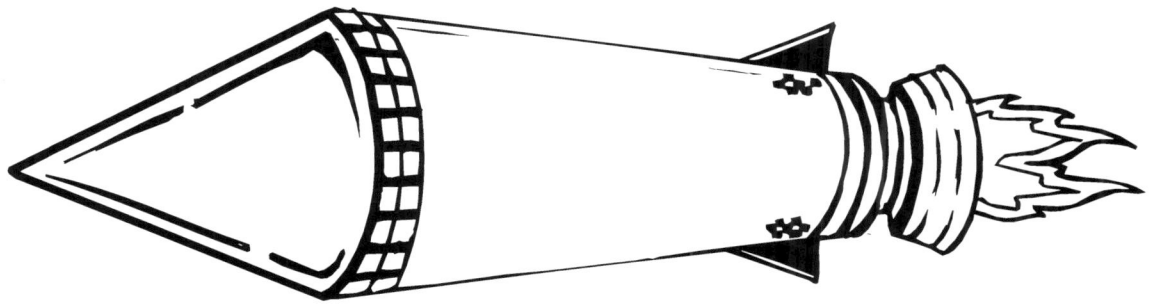

I beat the rocket:

Yes / No

🐾 Your friend guesses each letter in the word. He or she has 10 guesses before the rocket blasts off.

🐾 Write the correct guesses in the rocket.

🐾 Write the incorrect guesses in the boxes below.

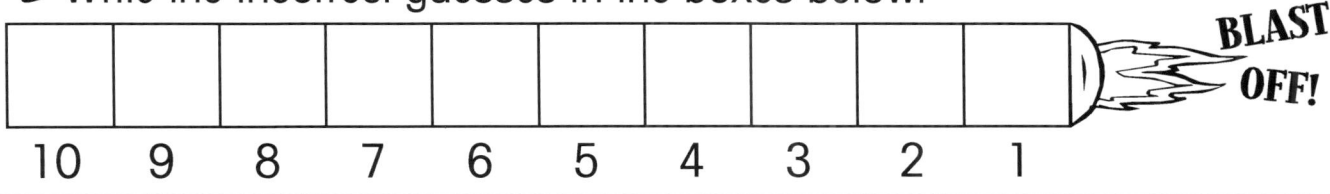

Prim-Ed Publishing ~ www.prim-ed.com

Activity 46 — Partner Testing

Name_____ My partner's name_____

1. Give your partner five spelling words.
2. Write the date and get ready for your test.
3. Your partner will slowly read each word twice.
4. When you are finished, read through your words again then hand them to your partner.
5. Your partner will mark your test, put on the score and hand it back to you.
6. Good luck!

Date_____

Total ☐

Activity 47 — Wordo!

🐾 Write your spelling words in the grid to play bingo with words.

50 Spelling Activities

Activity 48

Hello Hippo!

Play this game with a partner or in a small group.

- Write each spelling word on a card and cut out each of the pieces, including the hippo.
- Place all of the cards right way up on the playing surface.
- Choose one player to be the 'hippo hider'. The other players turn away while the 'hippo hider' hides the hippo under one of the cards.
- Each of the other players take turns to guess which word the hippo is under, then closing his or her eyes and spelling the word aloud. If the word is spelt correctly, the player turns over the card.
- The person to find the hippo says 'Hello Hippo!' and becomes the 'hippo hider' in the next game.

Activity 49 — Fish

- Write a spelling word on the back of each sea creature.
- Attach a paper clip to each creature and put them in a bucket.
- Use a 'fishing rod' made from a magnet on string tied to a stick or ruler to 'catch' fish in the bucket.
- Read and spell the word on the creature you caught.

Activity 50 — Snail Concentration

Play this game with a partner or in a small group.

- Cut out each snail card.
- Write each spelling word on the back of two cards.
- Place all cards face down on the playing surface.
- Take turns to turn over two cards, trying to find a match. When a match is found, the player picks up the cards and is allowed another turn.
- The winner is the person with the most pairs when no cards are left!

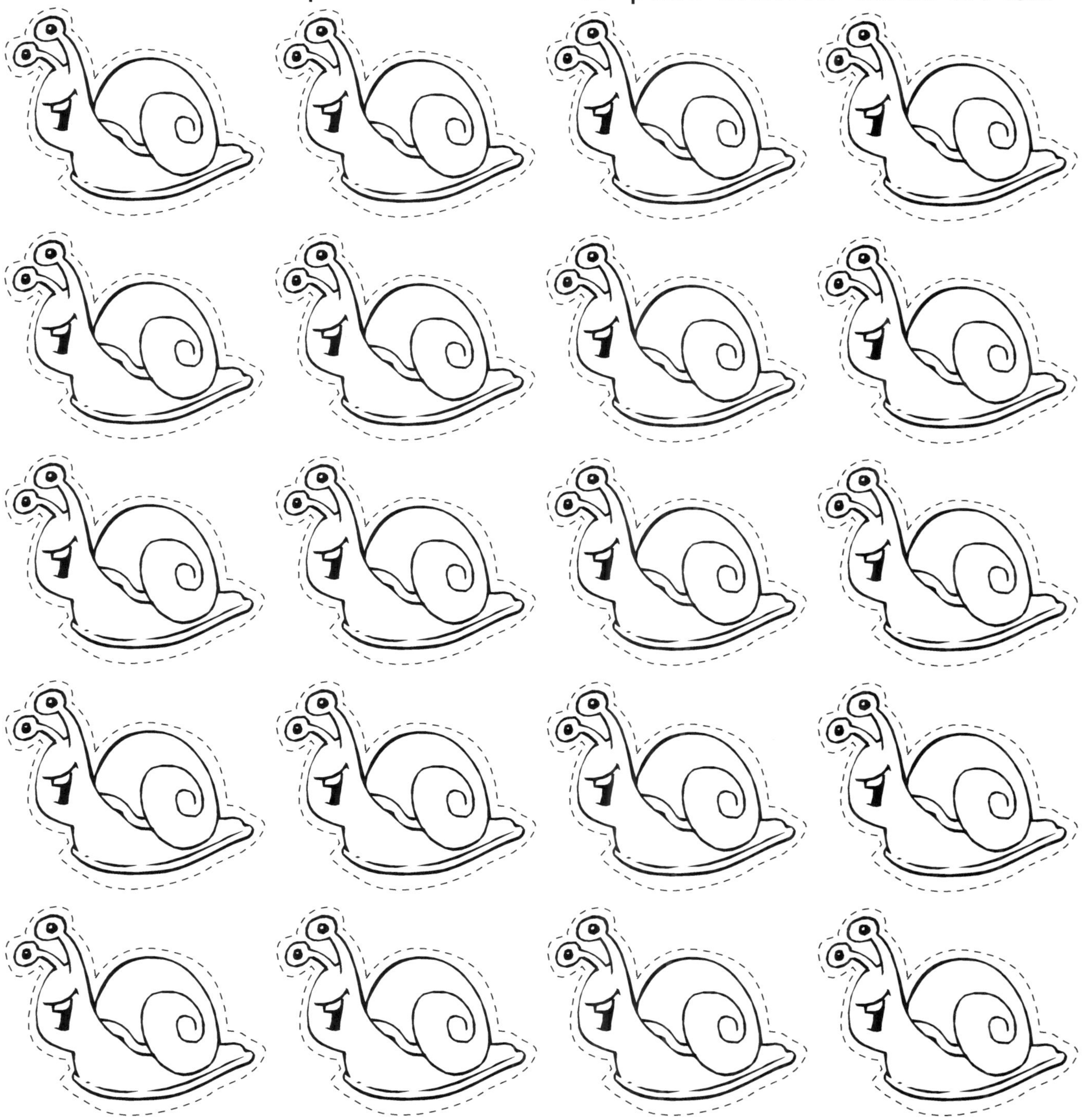

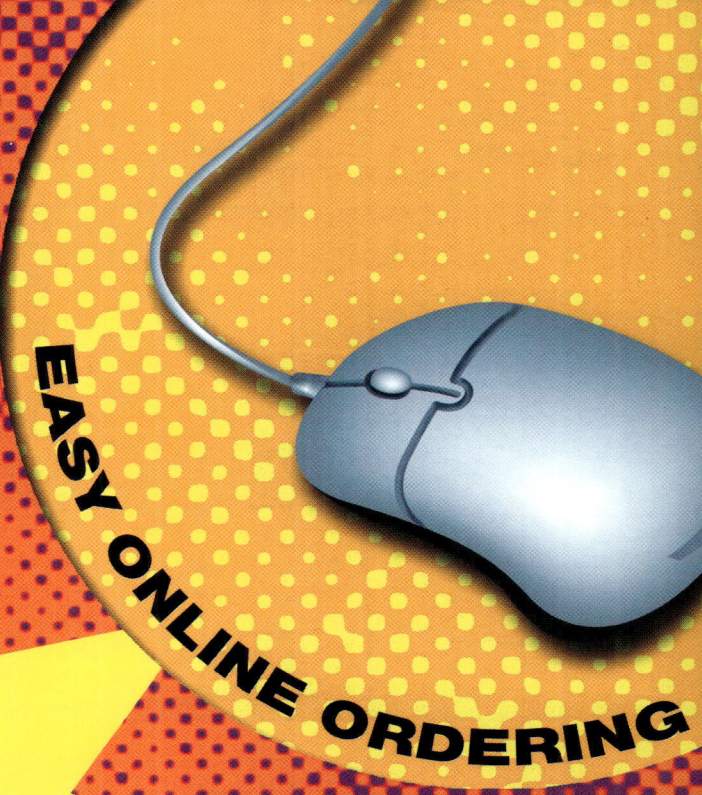